5. 17

ALTERNATIVE ENERGY

WIND
ENERGY

by Kris Woll

Content Consultant
Paul Stoy
Assistant Professor, Land Resources and
Environmental Sciences
Montana State University

Core Library

An Imprint of Abdo Publishing
abdopublishing.com

abdopublishing.com

Published by Abdo Publishing, a division of ABDO, PO Box 398166, Minneapolis, Minnesota 55439. Copyright © 2017 by Abdo Consulting Group, Inc. International copyrights reserved in all countries. No part of this book may be reproduced in any form without written permission from the publisher. Core Library™ is a trademark and logo of Abdo Publishing.

Printed in the United States of America, North Mankato, Minnesota
082016
012017

Cover Photo: Shutterstock Images
Interior Photos: Shutterstock Images, 1, 18, 35, 43; iStockphoto, 4; Diyana Dimitrova/ Shutterstock Images, 7; US Department of Energy, 9, 27; Bildagentur Zoonar GmbH/ Shutterstock Images, 10; Science & Society Picture Library/Getty Images, 12; Fedor Selivanov/ Shutterstock Images, 15; Tony Campbell/Shutterstock Images, 22; Gary Hincks/Science Source, 25; Bernhard Edmaier/Science Source, 30, 45; Ingo Wagner/Picture-Alliance/DPA/AP Images, 33; Julia Cumes/AP Images, 37; Patrick Pleul/Picture-Alliance/DPA/AP Images, 39

Editor: Arnold Ringstad
Series Designer: Nikki Farinella

Publisher's Cataloging-in-Publication Data

Names: Woll, Kris, author.
Title: Wind energy / by Kris Woll.
Description: Minneapolis, MN : Abdo Publishing, 2017. | Series: Alternative
    energy | Includes bibliographical references and index.
Identifiers: LCCN 2016945425 | ISBN 9781680784602 (lib. bdg.) |
    ISBN 9781680798456 (ebook)
Subjects: LCSH: Wind power--Juvenile literature. | Wind turbines--Juvenile
    literature. | Renewable energy sources--Juvenile literature.
Classification: DDC 621.4/5--dc23
LC record available at http://lccn.loc.gov/2016945425

CONTENTS

WHAT IS WIND POWER?

t is a windy night. You are 300 feet (91 m) above the ground in a tall, thin tower. Looking out a small window, you can see bright stars above. Around you, enormous blades slice through the air. A whooshing noise fills the tower. From outside, the wind turbine looks like a giant fan. It is generating electricity for the town below.

As long as the wind is blowing, turbines can generate electricity day or night.

Wind Farms

A wind farm is a large group of wind turbines. The turbines work together to produce power for communities and businesses. The rows of wind turbines are called arrays. The first wind farm was built in 1980 in New Hampshire. It had 20 wind turbines. Today wind farms are much larger. The biggest wind farm in the world is the Alta Wind Energy Center in California. It features more than 480 turbines.

Wind turbines sit on tall towers. They have two or three blades at the top. The wind causes these blades to spin. They turn the energy of the wind into electricity. This is wind power.

What Is Wind Power?

Wind energy is, in part, a form of a solar energy. The sun is always heating Earth's ground and air. Wind exists because of the temperature changes this creates. Some areas heat up. Others cool down. Warm air is less dense than cold air, so it rises. This movement helps create wind.

Workers may have to dangle high in the air when repairing large wind turbine blades.

The Earth spins on its axis as it orbits the sun. This spinning motion causes air to move. Wind turbines take advantage of all this motion. Wind propels the blades of a wind turbine to make electricity.

Big and Tall

Modern industrial wind turbines can be hundreds of feet tall. These turbines reach high above the ground. Up there the wind is stronger. The turbines of the future may reach even higher. Tall turbines are often tubes of steel. This shape and material makes them strong, yet light.

Benefits and Challenges

Wind energy is one of the fastest-growing energy sources. There are many reasons for this. Wind power is clean. Unlike coal and oil, it does not pollute when it is used. Wind is also easily available. In some places on the globe, the wind blows almost all the time. In addition, wind turbines do not take up much space. They can be built on a corner of a farm and still leave lots of land for planting.

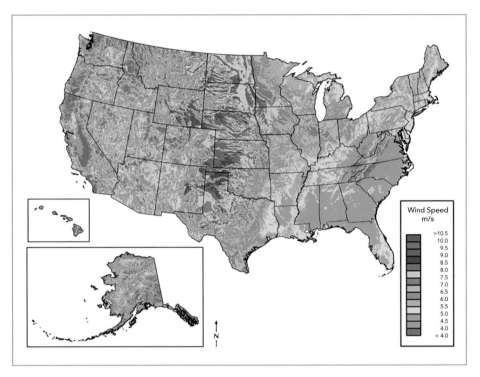

Where the Wind Blows

This map shows the average wind speeds across the United States at 262 feet (80 m) above the ground. Which areas have the strongest winds? Which areas have the least wind? What are the winds like where you live?

Wind energy is a promising technology, but it faces challenges. One challenge is bringing electricity from windy places to cities. Some of the windiest areas are far from the urban areas that use lots of electricity. In addition, setting up wind turbines can be very expensive. The wind is free, but turbines are not. Also, some people do not like the sound or look

Wind turbines sometimes pose a threat to birds that fly too close.

of wind turbines. There are environmental challenges, too. Turbines can pose a risk to some kinds of birds. Scientists, industries, government leaders, and communities are finding ways to overcome these challenges. They are also working together to make wind energy more affordable and effective. The wind turbines they are designing, building, and using are helping to change our energy future.

FURTHER EVIDENCE

Chapter One has a lot of information about the benefits and challenges of wind power. What is one of the main points of this chapter? What key evidence supports this point? Go to the article about wind energy at the website below. Find a quote from the website that supports the chapter's main point.

Onshore Wind Energy: What Are the Pros and Cons?

mycorelibrary.com/wind-energy

FABRICARE VN'ORGANO DEL QVALE LE
Trombe suonino, quando soffia il vento.
Theorema LXXVI.

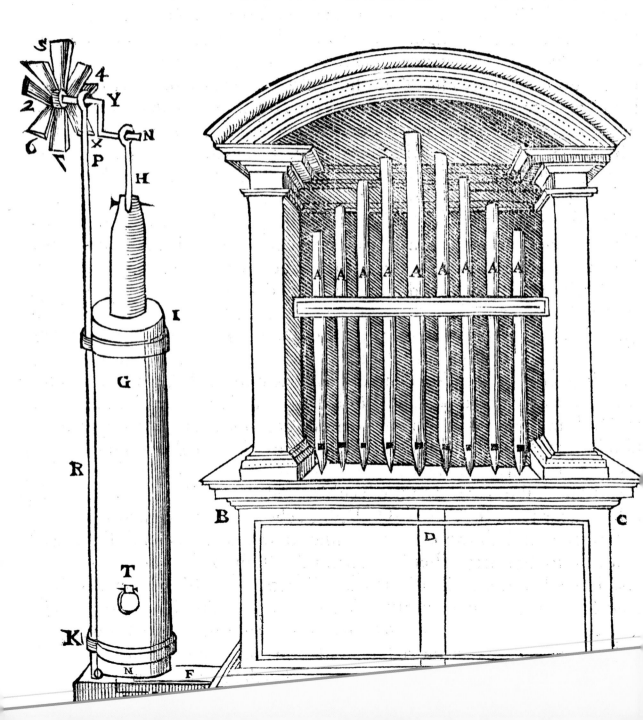

CHAPTER TWO

THE HISTORY OF WIND POWER

P eople have gotten power from the wind for thousands of years. Wind power dates back far before today's giant wind turbines. Wind has been harnessed to sail, drain, and mill. The use of wind for power is an important part of human history.

Early Wind Power

By 5000 BCE, the ancient Egyptians used wind to move their sailboats along the Nile River. A sail would

The ancient Greek inventor Hero of Alexandria developed a musical instrument powered by a small wind turbine.

catch the wind, and the wind's force would push the boat forward. Between 500 and 900 BCE, the Persians used wind power for water drainage and grain-milling. Early windmills were also used in ancient China for the same purposes. These early windmills worked similarly to modern turbines. The wind moved the windmill's sails. Then the sails turned a central shaft. Gears transferred this motion to grindstones or water pumps.

The Windmills of the Netherlands

Some of history's most famous windmills are in the Netherlands. Around 1390 CE, the first tower mills appeared in that part of Northern Europe.

Vertical and Horizontal

The earliest windmills were built with a vertical axis. This means they spun around like a merry-go-round. By the Middle Ages, post mills began to appear. These mills spun on a horizontal axis, like a Ferris wheel. They were mounted on posts, which explains their name. Most modern windmills and wind turbines spin on a horizontal axis. However, some cutting-edge designs have returned to the vertical style.

Many of the Netherlands' centuries-old windmills still stand today.

Many were used to drain water in low-lying areas. As with earlier mills, tower mills had sails that rotated in the wind. The sails moved a shaft, and the shaft moved the gears on pumps used to remove water. Draining water created new farming areas.

Tower mills had rooms inside for storing grain or other products. They also had a living space inside for a windsmith. The windsmith lived in the tower and controlled the sails, or blades. It was the windsmith's job to adjust the sails when the wind changed direction.

Over the next several hundred years, many kinds of windmills were built across the region. Some

Windmills Made History

Windmills in the Netherlands changed the area's history. Mills drained water from soggy land, making the soil suitable for farming. The mills powered the production of chalk, spices, and paper. Wind-powered sawmills turned trees into lumber for ships. One area with windmills, Kinderdijk, is especially well-known. People from all over the world travel there to see the historic mills.

were small and high above ground. Others were very large. Windmills were an important part of life in the Netherlands. They show up in many of the great works of art from this period.

Windmills in the American West

Windmills played a role in US history, too. They were an important power source as settlers moved west. In 1854 Daniel Halladay invented a windmill that could automatically turn in the direction of the wind. Soon windmills like these could be found on farms throughout the West. By harnessing the power of the wind to operate water pumps, settlers created large spaces for planting crops.

New innovations, such as steel blades, made the windmills strong enough to survive powerful winds. Advanced windmills were shown off at the 1893 World's Fair. This event was held in Chicago, Illinois. It lasted six months and attracted more than 27 million visitors. The fair featured exhibits on art, culture, and technology. The fair displayed windmills made

Small windmills were widely used in the American West.

by 15 companies. The windmill displays were very popular.

By the early 1900s, small wind turbines were creating electricity for individual homes and businesses. This was especially useful in remote areas. But interest in wind power soon slowed down. The United States created a power grid to supply electricity all across the country. Power lines were built not just in cities, but across the countryside as well. They carried electricity from large fossil fuel power plants to millions of homes. Individual families no longer needed to generate their own power.

Back to the Wind

Interest in wind returned later in the century. In the 1970s, the United States experienced an energy crisis. People were using large amounts of electricity and oil. The country experienced shortages of oil, and the price of energy spiked. Many worried that the availability of fossil fuels was unpredictable. Others were also concerned about fossil fuel pollution.

As a result, scientists, leaders, and citizens called for more renewable sources of energy. By 1978 President Jimmy Carter signed a law requiring that some energy must come from renewable sources. Wind was identified as one of these sources.

Research on wind energy skyrocketed. The development of newer wind turbines did, too. California led the way. It developed the first modern wind farms. Soon other places around the world followed. Wind power has continued to grow in the United States and abroad.

Concern about the environment and sustainability is not new. President Carter discussed US energy policy in a 1977 speech:

> *In order to conserve energy, the Congress is now acting to make automobiles, homes, and appliances more efficient, and to encourage industry to save both heat and electricity. . . .*
>
> *I hope that perhaps 100 years from now the change to inexhaustible energy sources will have been made, and our nation's concern about energy will be over. But we can make that transition smoothly—for our country and for our children and for our grandchildren—only if we take careful steps now to prepare ourselves for the future.*

> Source: Jimmy Carter. "Transcript of President's Address on Energy Problems." *New York Times. New York Times,* November 9, 1977. Web. Accessed April 26, 2016.

Consider Your Audience

Review this passage closely. Consider how you would change it if you were giving this speech today. Rewrite this information for the present-day audience. What would be the most effective form for sharing this message today? For example, would you give a speech, publish a letter in the newspaper, or write a blog post? How would your new approach differ from the original text, and why?

CHAPTER THREE

HOW WIND BECOMES POWER

Wind power may seem like a simple idea. But there are many scientific concepts at work when wind is turned into electricity. Wind power is made possible by climate science, physics, engineering, and more.

It Starts with the Sun

The science of wind power starts with the sun. In the day, the sun warms the air. At night, the air cools.

By heating Earth's atmosphere, the sun creates wind and is ultimately responsible for wind energy.

Cloud cover, the angle of the sunlight, and other factors change how much the sun heats different parts of the planet. Air over land warms faster than air over water, creating even more temperature differences. Warm air is light and rises. Cool air is dense and falls. Air falling and rising creates areas with different air pressure. The movement of air from areas of high pressure to areas of low pressure is what we call wind. The rotation of Earth also causes air to move, creating wind.

On the Move

The movement of wind is affected by the landscape, plants, and water in its way. High above the ground, wind blows very fast. It also moves fast in places where it can blow for long distances without anything getting in its way. Oceans and wide plains give the wind lots of room to blow.

The speed and direction of wind can be difficult to predict. Wind patterns change between seasons.

The movement of warm and cool air, along with the rotation of Earth, leads to winds that circulate air around the globe.

Wind Power and Wildlife

Research has shown that wind turbines can impact wildlife. Bats and birds can be injured or killed if they fly into moving turbine blades. Wind turbines may also interrupt migration patterns. Raptors and songbirds seem to be most affected by turbines. In addition, some ground birds may change their behavior in areas with many wind turbines. More research is needed to better understand why this is happening. Experts are looking for ways to allow both wind power and animal life to thrive.

Even over the course of a single day, the wind can vary significantly.

Making Electricity

Wind turbines turn the wind's kinetic energy into electricity. Kinetic energy is the energy of motion. When the wind strikes the blades of the turbine, the wind's energy is transferred to the blades. This causes the blades to spin. The blades are connected to a shaft. When the blades spin, the shaft spins along with them. The shaft goes into the wind turbine's nacelle. Inside the nacelle, the shaft spins within the generator. The generator uses a

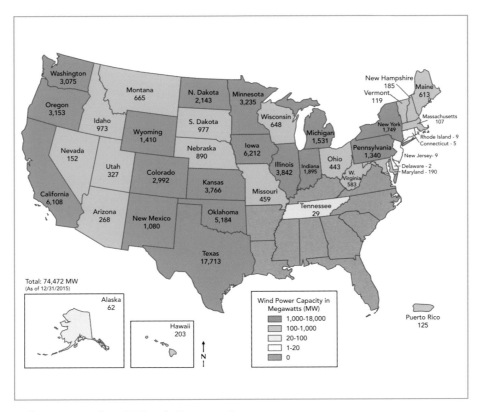

Total: 74,472 MW
(As of 12/31/2015)

Wind Power Capacity in Megawatts (MW)
- 1,000–18,000
- 100–1,000
- 20–100
- 1–20
- 0

Where Is the Wind Power?

The above map shows the installed wind power capacity in megawatts (MW), or millions of watts, by the end of 2015. Which areas produced the most wind power? Which areas did not produce any? Compare this map with the map of the windiest states in Chapter One. What do you notice about the two maps?

magnetic field to turn the energy of the spinning shaft into electricity.

The electricity is sent out through cables. It travels into the grid. Then it is distributed to customers. A typical wind turbine can produce enough electricity to power 225 to 300 homes. This number will likely increase as turbines improve.

Power to the People

Wind farms generate large amounts of electricity that can be sent through the power grid. As long as there is a path for the electricity to follow, the power can travel many miles to communities in need of electricity. Of course, sometimes the wind doesn't blow. On a calm day, a wind farm may produce little electricity. At those times, other sources of power are used to meet electricity needs.

Electric power is measured in watts and kilowatts. There are

Wind Turbines versus Windmills

What is the difference between a wind turbine and a windmill? Windmills power a specific piece of machinery. They may power a pump. They may grind grain. Wind turbines use the wind to generate electricity. This electricity can be used for a wide variety of tasks. Turbines power electrical systems that produce electricity for a single house, a community, or a power grid.

1,000 watts in one kilowatt. The amount of energy produced by wind turbines is often measured in kilowatt hours (kWh). One kWh is the production or use of 1,000 watts of electricity for one hour. For example, imagine a household oven uses 1,000 watts when it is on. If it is turned on for one hour, it has used up one kWh. A large wind turbine can generate as many as 6 million kWh of electricity each year.

EXPLORE ONLINE

Modern wind turbines have many mechanical parts that turn the wind into power. The graphic on the below website shows a wind turbine at work. It explains how all the parts work together. How does this animation help you better understand how wind turbines do their work?

What's Inside a Wind Turbine?

mycorelibrary.com/wind-energy

CHAPTER FOUR

THE FUTURE OF WIND POWER

Today approximately 4 percent of the electricity in the United States is produced by the wind. Two states, South Dakota and Iowa, get more than 25 percent of their electricity from the wind. The US Department of Energy estimates that more than 20 percent of the country's energy could someday be provided by wind.

Enormous wind farms are beginning to generate large portions of the electricity in many states.

How will we get there? Scientists continue to research more efficient ways of producing wind power. Turbine designers are creating longer, lighter blades. These design changes make it possible to produce more electricity from a single turbine.

In addition, more wind turbines will need to be put to use. Some of these may be on a small or local scale. They may follow the example of the University of Minnesota, Morris, which constructed a 230-foot (70-m) turbine

Workers carefully craft each blade to make it cut through the air as efficiently as possible.

in 2005. This turbine now produces about half of the university's power. Other new turbines might be much larger. Not all of them will be on land.

Wind on the Water

Interest in developing offshore wind farms is growing in the United States and around the world. Offshore wind farms currently exist in many countries, including the United Kingdom and Denmark. These wind farms can make use of the strong winds that often blow over ocean water. They also do not use up space on land.

The wind turbines used in offshore wind farms are generally even bigger than the ones found on land. Offshore wind turbines are usually built around 5 to 15 miles (8 to 24 km) from the coast. This decreases their impact on the natural beauty of the landscape. Underwater cables connect offshore wind farms to the coast.

Offshore wind farms are being built in windy coastal areas around the world.

Offshore Wind Farms in the United States

The United States Department of Energy is supporting additional research and development in offshore wind power. In 2016 the first US offshore wind farm was under construction off the coast of Rhode Island. The designers planned to include five wind turbines, powering more than 17,000 homes.

But not everyone supports offshore wind. Building offshore wind farms is expensive. It also requires drilling into the sea floor to construct the platforms. This drilling can impact sea life. Other people oppose offshore wind farms because they do not like the appearance. Some planned offshore wind farms in the United States have not worked out. High costs and concerns from local communities have resulted in delays or cancellations.

Global Wind

Interest in wind energy is growing all around the world. China installed its first wind turbines less

Offshore wind supporters and opponents made their voices heard in a 2010 demonstration in Massachusetts.

than 15 years ago. Today it has the world's largest wind power capacity. In Brazil, wind power is the fastest-growing source of electricity. Wind power currently accounts for most of the renewable energy produced in India. In Ethiopia's rainy season, much of the country's clean energy comes from hydroelectric power. But large wind farms provide clean energy when the weather is dry. In 2013 Denmark reported that it got 28 percent of its electricity from wind

A Town Fueled by Wind

The island of Samso, Denmark, has achieved a remarkable goal. It gets 100 percent of its energy from local wind power. Samso has about 4,000 residents who live in 22 separate small villages. It is also home to 21 wind turbines. Some are built on land and some are offshore. Samso residents use about 26 million kWh of electricity each year. Their wind turbines supply more than enough energy for the island. Samso exports electricity to other parts of Denmark and nearby countries.

The growing wind industry will need many new engineers and other workers.

power. It plans to get at least half of all its electricity from wind by 2020.

The Winds of Change

Wind is a clean, renewable energy source. It has been a part of our past, and it is now a major source of power all around the world. It is a compelling alternative to fossil fuels, such as coal and oil. Scientists, entrepreneurs, and government leaders continue to work on ways to use wind power to benefit more people. Vast wind farms with tall turbines will likely be an important part of our energy future.

Steven Vietor, a technician and wind technology instructor, shared his reflections on the view from the top of a turbine:

> When you look out, how small everything you are familiar with looks! You feel happy to be part of a very special group of women and men who build and maintain the wind turbines that provide such a clean energy source for all of us.
>
> Wind technicians don't always climb out on top of the nacelle but every time I do, I poke my head through the top hatch to see the view. Sometimes we work late. At night I will watch all the other wind turbines with their flashing lights against the night sky. . . . The turbines are all making electricity to power your nightlights while you sleep. I wish everyone could sit next to me on top of that turbine and watch!

Source: Steven Vietor. Personal Interview. E-mail. March 20, 2016.

Point of View

The speaker in this passage is describing his own experience. He has a very favorable view of wind turbines. Would you like to take in the view from the top of the nacelle? Why or why not? Do you agree with the speaker's favorable impressions of wind turbines at work?

- Wind is a form of solar energy.
- In a wind turbine, wind pushes blades, causing a shaft to spin inside a generator. The generator turns this motion into electricity.
- Wind energy is one of the fastest-growing sources of energy in the world today.
- Modern wind turbines can be hundreds of feet tall.
- Wind was used for power in ancient Egypt and ancient China.
- Windmills played an important role in the history of the Netherlands.
- Windmills were key energy sources in the American West.
- After losing popularity in the early 1900s, interest in wind energy began to soar during the energy crisis of the 1970s.
- Many of the windiest states are in the center of the United States, an area known as the Great Plains.

- By 2016, South Dakota and Iowa got more than 25 percent of their energy from wind power.
- Many offshore wind farms exist in Europe.
- The island of Samso, Denmark, gets 100 percent of its energy from wind power.

STOP AND THINK

Take a Stand

Some people think the next developments in wind energy will happen offshore. But some communities on coastlines have opposed the building of these wind farms. They may support wind power but do not want the large turbines blocking their view. How do you think the locations for wind farms should be selected? Which is more important: preserving the current landscape or building more wind turbines? Why?

Another View

Sources can have different points of view. This book talks about wind energy as a clean, renewable source of energy. Ask a librarian or teacher to help you locate another source on this topic, and take time to read it. Then write a short essay comparing and contrasting the point of view of that source to the one in this book. Are they similar or different? In what ways?

Surprise Me

Chapter Two tells the story of wind energy's history. What are three facts that you found surprising about this history? Write a few sentences about each surprising fact. Why did these facts surprise you?

Say What?

Learning about wind energy can mean learning a lot of new words. Write down five words from this book that are new to you. Use a dictionary to learn about their meaning. In your own words, write a definition for each of them.

GLOSSARY

array
a group of wind turbines

fossil fuels
sources of energy that
come from the remains of
prehistoric plants and animals

generator
a machine that turns
mechanical energy into
electricity

hydroelectric power
electricity generated using
the motion of rushing water

kilowatt
1,000 watts of electricity

kinetic energy
a form of energy that an
object has because of its
motion

nacelle
an enclosed space containing
the mechanical parts of a
wind turbine

offshore
not on land; in the water
along a shoreline

renewable energy
energy collected from
sources that do not run out

wind turbine
a machine with spinning
blades that turns wind energy
into electricity

LEARN MORE

Books

Friedman, Mark. *What Does It Do? Windmill*. Ann Arbor, MI: Cherry Lake Publishing, 2012.

Kamkwamba, William and Bryan Mealer. *The Boy Who Harnessed the Wind*. New York: Dial Books, 2015.

Kopp, Megan. *Energy from Wind: Wind Farming*. New York: Crabtree Publishing, 2016.

Websites

To learn more about Alternative Energy, visit **booklinks.abdopublishing.com**. These links are routinely monitored and updated to provide the most current information available.

Visit **mycorelibrary.com** for free additional tools for teachers and students.

INDEX

ABOUT THE AUTHOR

Kris Woll is a Minneapolis-based writer and editor.